SERIOUSLY SEEKING GOD

A Four-Week Study
on Contemplating the Parables

By Suzan Phillips

South Carolina United Methodist Advocate Press

Advocate Press

South Carolina United Methodist Advocate Press, Columbia, South Carolina

Copyright © 2024 by South Carolina United Methodist Advocate Press

First published in the United States of America in 2024
by the South Carolina United Methodist Advocate Press.

Library of Congress Cataloging-in-Publication Data
Seriously Seeking God
p. cm.

Cover photo: kieferpix

ISBN 979-8-9883575-5-1

Dedication

To my dear husband, Charles, and your
undying support and steadfast love.

Introduction

You've read the parables and heard them preached and taught many times, I'm sure. They are well-known, and because they are known so well, we often take them for granted and believe we have nothing more to learn from them.

This study seeks to take you deep down into the parable in order to hear what new thing Jesus is saying to us. Out of a contention that God speaks because God is present and active with us in this moment, we will spend a week on an individual parable, listening to it and wrestling with it. What is God revealing to my heart? What word or image or character or human trait or human condition leaps off the page at me? What stays with me throughout the week?1 We will pray for God to show us what we need to see and hear, again, out of the contention that God is present and seeks to reach us.

Throughout this week of focused and intentional contemplation on the parables of Jesus, we will arrive at our own individual observations and questions, which may or may not overlap with others or with what we have heard before.

This study is grounded in two fundamental truths without which your participation in this study will conclude in stagnation.

The first truth is about God. God is active and present. God unceasingly reaches out to the heart that intentionally and willingly reaches out to God in a relationship. God communicates. And God loves. God desires a close and deep connection to such a heart and desires that heart to grow and to change so that we can bring God's love here on earth—to move us out of our complacency into a dynamic, thriving, abundant wholeness for ourselves and for

---

1. A kind of *Lectio Divina*.

others—indeed, for the entire world. Furthermore, God knows the intimate, secret, hidden parts of our hearts and our consciousness. Not only does God know us, but God accesses our hearts and our consciousness.

The second truth is about prayer. A sincere and intentional prayer, spoken in absolute and whole-hearted expectation—out of a knowledge of God's activity and love—reaches God. Furthermore and most integral, God responds to this kind of genuine prayer. This is not a prayer of hope or wishing; rather, this is a prayer of expectation that God is near and active, waiting for us to come to God.

Also integral to this study and the prayer that will undergird this journey through the parables (and any further growth) is your most sincere desire to see inside yourself. It's a desire to learn and to grow and, in a positive and healthy way, to change. This is a prayer of surrender and vulnerability in order to see inside ourselves and for God to show us. In fact, this is the process of repentance.

So we will take on this process of repentance through the study and contemplation of the parables.

What is a parable?

A parable is a story that uses the literary devices of allegory, simile, or metaphor. An allegory "speak[s] one thing and signifies something other than what is said,"[2] while a simile is when we say this thing is like that thing. A good example of a metaphor is Jesus saying that he is the Lamb of God; the comparison is communicated in a very close way. Jesus is the bread of life. The Lord is my shepherd.

In each case, two things are placed alongside each other. We talk about one thing in terms of the other. One way of understanding this comparison is to say that it is an "interaction of meaning" between what you know and what you don't know.[3] The meaning of the known, physical, tangible thing is transferred to the unknown, spiritual, intangible thing in order to communicate and teach the unknown spiritual reality. For example, Jesus is the bread of life. We know bread literally and physically. And what we know about it is that it feeds us, sustains our life, nourishes our bodies, and satisfies our hunger. So to think of Jesus as bread, then, is to think of him in the same way but not

---

2. E. A. Livingstone, ed., *The Oxford Concise Dictionary of the Christian Church*, 3rd ed (Oxford: Oxford University Press, 2013), 15.

3. Susan V. Gallagher and Roger Lundin, *Literature through the Eyes of Faith* (San Francisco: Harper, 1989).

physically, not literally. We take what we know about the physical to teach us about the spiritual: Jesus is our spiritual food and sustenance. And in the parables, most of the time, the unknown spiritual reality that Jesus wants to teach us about is the kingdom of Heaven.

According to Eerdman's Dictionary, *parabole* was used in the New Testament to identify a variety of literary forms. Literally the word signifies something cast alongside another thing to clarify it, [and] the Gospels are not consistent in what they describe as a parable."[4] Today there is no common agreement among scholars on what a parable is or how it functions. Parables are read in many different ways: as allegories, as stories with a religious moral, as examples of Christian morality, as metaphors, as stories that refract a particular understanding of human existence, and as political and economic stories.[5] Also interestingly, parables were an ancient storytelling structure found in Old Testament and Jewish life. We must remember that the comparison is not always one for one, not always easy. In fact, the word "parable" can also mean "riddle."[6] Parables are meant to make the audience think and to challenge them. But since they were commonly used throughout the Hebrew world, the audience would expect the story structure to follow a familiar pattern, and they would be very familiar with the Old Testament allusions, which we often miss.

So why did Jesus teach in parables? He tells us in Mark 4:10-12 (NIV): "When he was alone, the Twelve and the others around him asked him about the parables. He told them, 'The secret of the kingdom of God has been given to you. But to those on the outside everything is said in parables so that, 'they may be ever seeing but never perceiving, and ever hearing but never understanding; otherwise they might turn and be forgiven!'"

We find this also in Mathew 13:10-15, Luke 8:9-10, Matthew 13:34-35, and Mark 4:33-34.

In each of these examples, we hear Jesus say he uses parables so that the people "on the outside" will "never understand." Jesus quotes Isaiah, which the audience would recognize as coming from Isaiah 6:9-10, and they would know its context. In it, the prophet sees God on the throne of the temple, and the prophet's tongue is touched with a coal, at which time he is cleansed.

4. David Noel Freedman, Allen C. Myers, and Astrid B. Beck, eds. *Eerdman's Dictionary of the Bible* (Grand Rapids, Mich.: Wm. B. Eerdman's, 2000). Accordance Bible Software, https://www.accordance-bible.com

5. Freedman, *Eerdman's*.

6. Toni Craven and Walter Harrelson, "The Psalms" in *The New Interpreter's Study Bible* (Nashville: Abingdon, 2003), 820.

God then asks: "Whom shall I send?" Isaiah answers: "Here am I; Send me" (6:8 NRSV). Isaiah willingly volunteers; then God instructs the prophet to keep telling the people and predicts that they will not hear or perceive. They will instead, "ever see … ever hear … but never perceive."It's about the heart.

Jesus's words here can seem confusing, but perhaps we can see that those who have been "given" the "secrets of the kingdom"—the disciples—are like Isaiah; they are willing, in contrast to those on the outside, who are not willing. Furthermore, I contend that those on the inside who do hear and understand are not only willing, but their heart is different from those on the outside. Those who have been given the "mysteries of the kingdom," who do perceive and understand, have a different kind of heart. This is because they are willing and present and curious and engaged and attentive and have seen something in Jesus that has caused them to give up their lives and follow him—is it faith? Because of these things, we see an open heart and mind, a willing spirit, a trust, a surrender.

And note that these mysteries are "given," a passive verb, meaning that these insiders did not grab or manipulate or control this understanding. Rather, they are recipients of a gift. Why? They have spent time and energy with Jesus; they have given themselves and given their hearts. God's mysteries taught by Jesus in the parables are understood by those who willingly spend time and energy in trust: they say, "Here I am. Send me," like Isaiah.

This idea of the giving of the understanding points directly to the Holy Spirit's activity. And we see here that the willing and open heart that surrenders to Jesus in trust and faith receives blessing, a gift: to understand the mysteries of the kingdom of heaven. They are given the ability to grasp God's love and forgiveness, and their response is repentance. Like Isaiah, they place themselves in God's presence willingly in surrender, and they are cleansed, saved, forgiven, redeemed—all of these. This response of repentance demonstrates a transformation into a new heart.

We can imagine it as an equation or a process: Hear about Jesus; listen to message; choose to know more; give your time and energy; study; pray; surrender, trust; open your heart; receive God's love; recognize sin; repent; respond with "send me." We hear a similar process from John Wesley. According to Wesley, the founder of Methodism, the Holy Spirit is "God's gracious empowering presence"[7] that transforms our hearts by "enlightening our un-

---

7. Mark K. Olson, "John Wesley's Doctrine of the Holy Spirit." Wesleyscholar.com, accessed April 1, 2023, https://wesleyscholar.com/john-wesleys-doctrine-of-the-holy-spirit/.

derstandings, rectifying our wills and affections, renewing our natures, uniting our persons to Christ, assuring us of [our] adoption ..., leading us in our actions, purifying and sanctifying our souls and bodies."[8] Wesley continues to claim that the Spirit accomplishes these changes by "the saving message of Holy Scripture being perceived and experienced through graciously restored spiritual senses."[9] So we can see that Wesley also claims that the Spirit works in our hearts to change us, and that it is the understanding of scripture that accommodates this change. This understanding, or perception, of the "saving message" is given to us who have a "rectified will and affection" and a "renew[ed] nature," who are "purified and sanctified." The Spirit then "leads our actions"—or leads us to say, "Send me." The Spirit has both called us to change and effected our change. We have been willing and have given our heart to this activity.

But what are we talking about when we say "heart?"

In Greek, the heart is *kardia*—the seat of all emotions, intellect, spirit, the deepest part of the self, the soul. According to scholar Daniel R. Goodman, "Καρδία stands for the mind, the inner man ... the subject or seat, not only of the affections, but of thought, imagination, meditation, memory, perception, reflection, knowledge, skill, belief, judgment, reasoning, consciousness."[10]

In Hebrew, the meaning is the same: *Lev* = heart = *kardia*. As Goodman explains, "The inner man in contrast with outer; the inner man, the soul, comprehending mind, affections and will; specific reference to mind: knowledge; thinking, reflection; inclinations, resolutions and determinations of the will; moral character; conscience. The seat of appetites, emotions, passions, joy, courage."[11]

In both Hebrew and Greek understanding, the heart is the entirety of a person; nothing is held back or left out. So giving this deep part of the self is no small matter. Opening this part of yourself is no small matter. It can only be done in total trust. And this is the kind of heart that God blesses. This kind of heart is the new that God makes possible. From this new heart, like Jesus, we, too, will understand the "mysteries of the kingdom" of God because God will pour this love into our open and newly transformed heart.

Those on the outside, however, will hear with their ears and see with their

---

8. Olson, "John Wesley's Doctrine of the Holy Spirit."

9. Olson, "John Wesley's Doctrine of the Holy Spirit."

10. Daniel R. Goodman, "On the Use of בַל and Καρδία in the Old and New Testaments," *Journal of the Society of Biblical Literature and Exegesis*, no. X. (Jun-Dec 1881): 67-72.

11. H. F. W. Gesenius, *A Hebrew and English Lexicon of the Old Testament*, ed. Francis Brown (Oxford: Oxford University Press, 1952). Accordance Bible Software, https://accordancebible.com.

eyes but never perceive the mysteries. This person has a closed heart, does not know God, and does not trust God.

There is a slight difference between hearing and listening, between seeing and perceiving. This difference is the difference between the insider and the outsider. As Jesus quotes Isaiah, who was sent to wicked Israel who did not turn and repent, Jesus's words imply that he does not want the closed heart on the outside to "turn and be forgiven." Rather, Jesus wants the heart that is willing to repent, not the closed heart with a selfish motive. If Jesus told the secrets to God's kingdom not in these kinds of riddles or parables, the kind where even the wicked sinner with a heart closed to God could perceive the mystery, then repentance would lose its significance. It would no longer be a surrender of self, a willingness to see and admit sin and then to change. Instead, it would be merely a tool for admittance into heaven, a tool for saving the self. Jesus is after change of heart. Such a false repentance would not be rooted in a changed heart.

You have a willing and open heart; that is why you are reading this study. You have trust. You are on the "inside." But this trust and openness and curiosity all are on a continuum or a spectrum. These traits are not all or nothing. This study seeks to move us along that continuum to a deeper and more intimate connection to the "mysteries" of God's love and God's kingdom.

Parables may speak to people differently, and we do not need what Amy-Jill Levine calls a "special key to unlock a singular meaning; rather they challenge us to look into the hidden aspects of our own values and lives."12 These hidden aspects of our lives could be different for each of us. We are unique; each of us will see and hear what we need to see and hear. Indeed, we go to this task with the understanding that God speaks to us through scripture, and because God knows us intimately, God shows us what we each need to hear or see. Spending time in study and prayer will reveal more and more, even in these well-known stories.

Themes

As we study the parables, we will hear Jesus teach mostly about the kingdom of heaven or kingdom of God and who God is.

Jesus is also very interested in relationships: father/son, mother/daughter, manager/worker, husband/wife, leaders/community. How do we treat those

---

12. Amy-Jill Levine, *Short Stories by Jesus: The Enigmatic Parables of a Controversial Rabbi* (New York: Harper One, 2014), 3.

we love? How do we treat each other? How do the powerful treat the power-less?

Jesus is also interested in our priorities. What do we find important? Who do we put first? Jesus pushes us to examine why we make these choices. But Jesus is also teaching us about celebration and banquets, tables, and food.

God rejoices when we change.

Gospel parallels

Some of the parables appear in each of the synoptic gospels: Matthew, Mark, and Luke. Each writer treats the parable a bit differently, however. We will take note of those differences, where sometimes it will slightly alter our interpretation. Each writer has a different approach to the parables. For example, Matthew worries about scripture fulfillment, while Luke wants to interpret and soften. They both expand the parable more than Mark. Notice, too, that the fourth gospel, John, has no parables. Another interesting differ-ence is sometimes the placement within the action of the story. Sometimes their location in the story can impact our understanding.

They still speak to us, but the meaning might seem different.

These "enigmatic" stories still speak to us today, even though we are not first-century Palestinian Jews. The voice of Jesus is still active and reaching into human hearts today. The stories and characters are timeless. However, we need to be aware that we often make them too simplistic or moralistic—like a children's sermon. In his genius, Jesus goes much deeper than that. He in-tends to provoke and challenge us, not necessarily to comfort us. Remember, he wants our hearts to change, so he will prick our hearts and force us to look at ourselves so that we can change, if we are willing. He will reveal who we are as he confronts, challenges, and disturbs us. We can see, now, why some stay on the "outside," for they cannot or choose not to confront their choices and pains and sins, and the parables challenge us to look into those hidden parts of our own selves and lives. Doing so can be very difficult. So some continue to hear and not listen, see and not perceive. Have you ever done that?

Jesus will also show us God's character.

Process

Use a study Bible as you do this study; I recommend The New Interpreter's Study Bible. Doing so will aid in understanding the context and the Old Testament allusions.

Our goal for this study is as follows:
- To listen
- To grow
- Not to declare the "correct" interpretation
- To ask: what is God saying to me?
- To practice reading scripture closely

Our process, grounded in prayer and expectation, is as follows:
- Pray: God, show my open heart and willing spirit what I need to see and hear so I can grow closer to you and bring your kingdom on earth as it is in Heaven.
- Read the parable.
- Read again. Do a close reading: underline, highlight, take notes, draw pictures.
- Pay attention to the verbs, the characters, the setting, what came just before this parable. and what comes after the parable.
- Ask questions.
- Notice the differences between the gospels.
- Read again (maybe out loud).
- Read again.
- Pray.
- Look at images or pictures or artwork of the story (not anything else online).
- What word or image is speaking to you? Write it down.
- Pray.
- Ask: Where has God taken me today? Write it down.

You can read throughout the week or do these readings all at the same time.

Practice the process

Now let's practice this process with this compact parable of the seed growing secretly, only found in Mark 4:26-29.

> He also said, "The kingdom of God is as if someone would scatter seed on the ground, and would sleep and rise night and day, and the seed would sprout and grow, he does not know how. The earth produces of itself, first the stalk, then the head, then the full grain in the

head. But when the grain is ripe, at once he goes in with his sickle, because the harvest has come."

Some observations from a close reading:
- A process
- The earth produces of itself – inherently – the ripening is sure
- Creation
- "He does not know how"
- The someone who scattered is not in control but participates in this inherent process
- The combination of elements: seed, earth, sower
- Results: in abundance, harvest, nourishment and food
- The scatterer gets the harvest, the nourishment

Questions:
- What do I think about the word kingdom?
- What is the seed?
- What is Jesus telling us?
- We can say: I don't know.

What I saw, heard:
- Jesus is telling us that God is reliable
- Faithful
- Present
- At work even if I don't see it or understand it
- God's work results in life-giving goodness
- The goodness is a gift
- God does it; we don't. But we participate. We go and scatter in the same way.

We will practice this process each week with a different parable. You should have some notes or drawings, questions, thoughts, and conclusions written down. Wrestle with the comparison that the parable uses; really think and pray. Try to "hear" what Jesus is teaching about the kingdom of God or God's realm. Let the story roll around in your head all week. Try to envision the action and the characters, remembering that it is a comparison between the known and the unknown. You might try making a list of the known and the unknown.

In our above example, the knowns are the garden, the seed, the sower, and the harvest. And like those known things, God's kingdom produces a harvest, for example. It's not a harvest of food, but a harvest of love.

Follow the agenda below each week. At the end of the week, you will read the discussion in this book on the parable. This daily reading and studying plan will walk you through a close reading with questions to stir thinking and exploration.

Our read and study plan for each week

Each day, spend at least twenty or thirty minutes for the daily reading and praying. You will need a notebook, pencil, and Bible. Try to answer the day's questions in your notebook as completely as you can. Nothing formal. Just your own thoughts. Do not worry about correct answers or interpretations. Just focus on listening. What is God saying to me today?

Sometimes, our answer is: "I don't know." That's okay. This is a process.

Throughout your day, think about what you've read and continue to pray for insights. Continue to ruminate on the parable, allowing it to roll around in your head and thoughts.

Each week will follow this basic pattern:

Monday: Pray for an open, listening heart. Then, in expectation, read the parable at least once. Close the Bible and sit quietly in contemplation of what you just read. Maybe draw a picture or sketch of the parable during this quiet contemplation. Or maybe search images of the parable. For example, search images of different kinds of seeds, etc. But only search images, no commentaries, etc.

Tuesday: Begin with prayer. Again, in expectation, read the parable at least once, maybe out loud. If the parable appears in more than one gospel, read each version. Pay attention to the differences and similarities. Underline or highlight what you notice. Do these differences alter the parable? Write down your answer. What do you think is being compared? What do your Bible footnotes say about the parable? Does this information add to your thoughts on the parable? Sit quietly in contemplation of this exercise.

Wednesday: Begin with prayer and expectation. Read the parable. Today, notice what action precedes the parable. Is this information helpful? In what way? Now, notice the action that follows the parable. Is this action tied to the parable in any way? Does the location of the parable impact your understanding? Do you see it in a new way, or does it alter the meaning at all? Is the location the same in each version? How are they different? Then sit quietly in contemplation of this exercise.

Thursday: As always, begin with the prayer for an open, listening heart. In expectation, read the parable. Let's look at the characters. Who are they? Notice what each character says. What do they do? Can you identify the motives for their actions? Why do you think they do what they do and say what they say? What else do you notice about each character? Now look at the setting of the parable. Where does the action take place? Why do you think Jesus uses this setting? The commentary in your study Bible may help. Next, where do you notice conflict or tension? Now, sit quietly in contemplation of this exercise.

Friday: Begin with prayer. Read the parable. Look back over your notes from the week. What do you hear after this week's study? What is this parable teaching you? Some things to consider: Which character do you seem to focus on the most? Can you answer why? What does this parable tell you about who God is? What does this parable tell you about what matters to God? What does this parable tell you about how God's kingdom operates? Sit in quiet contemplation of these questions. Maybe draw a picture or write down a word that seems to speak to you. What is God revealing to you?

Saturday: As always, begin with prayer. First, read the "Discussion" section in the chapter. Then, reflect on your week's notes and the discussion. Write down your thoughts, observations, questions, and concerns. Finally, what do you feel that God is revealing to you in this parable?

Sunday: Rest and pray in quiet contemplation of the parable.

Let's begin.

Chapter One
The Sower

Matthew 13:1-9, 18-23; Mark 4:1-9, 13-20;
Luke 8:4-8, 11-15

Step One: Follow the "Read and Study" plan for the week:

Monday: Pray for an open, listening heart. Then, in expectation, read the parable at least once. Close the Bible and sit quietly in contemplation of what you just read. Maybe draw a picture or sketch of the parable during this quiet contemplation. Or maybe search images of the parable. But only search images, no commentaries, etc.

Tuesday: Pray for an open, listening heart. Again, in expectation, read the parable at least once, maybe out loud. If the parable appears in more than one gospel, read each version. Pay attention to the differences and similarities. Underline or highlight what you notice. Do these differences alter the parable? Write down your answer. What do you think is being compared? What do your Bible footnotes say about the parable? Does this information add to your thoughts on the parable? Sit quietly in contemplation of this exercise.

Wednesday: Begin with prayer and expectation. Read the parable. Today, notice what action precedes the parable. Is this information helpful? In what way? Now, notice the action that follows the parable. Is this action tied to the parable in any way? Does the location of the parable impact your understanding? Do you see it in a new way, or does it alter the meaning at all? Is the location the same in each version? How are they different? Then, sit quietly in contemplation of this exercise.

Thursday: As always, begin with the prayer for an open, listening heart. In expectation, read the parable. Let's look at the characters. Who are they? Notice what each character says. What do they do? Can you identify the motives for their actions? Why do you think they do what they do and say what they say? What else do you notice about each character? Now, look at the setting of the parable. Where does the action take place? Why do you think Jesus uses this setting? The commentary in your study Bible may help. Next, where do you notice conflict or tension? Now, sit quietly in contemplation.

Friday: Begin with prayer, as usual. Read the parable. Look back over your notes from the week. What do you hear after this week's study? What is this parable teaching you? Some things to consider: Which character do you seem to focus on the most? Can you answer why? What does this parable tell you about who God is? What does this parable tell you about what matters to God? What does this parable tell you about how God's kingdom operates? Sit in quiet contemplation of these questions. Maybe draw a picture or write down a word that seems to speak to you. What is God revealing to you?

Saturday: After your prayer of expectation and surrender, and after having spent the week reading, thinking, praying, and listening to this parable, read the following discussion. Perhaps you will gain more clarity or affirmation, or maybe something else will arise for you. Write down your thoughts, observations, questions, and concerns. Finally, what do you feel that God is revealing to you in this parable?

Sunday: Rest and pray in quiet contemplation of the parable.

Step Two: Discussion

Did you notice that Luke places this parable as an answer to the question, "What can be compared to the kingdom of God?" Jesus answers with the parable of the sower and says, "Let those with ears listen and hear."

We see right away that the theme in this parable is people who listen. The parable begins and ends with this word, "listen." It is an action, a turning of attention, a giving of self to let this story work through your understanding and intellect. More than mere hearing, listening equates to something deeper, more like comprehension. Jesus teaches by using a *parabolé*, which is a comparison.[1] Comparisons use what we know and likens it to what we don't know. This side-by-side comparison illumines the unknown thing.

In the parable of the sower, Jesus illumines the different ways people re-

---

1. Aaron M. Gale, "The Gospel According to Matthew" in *The Jewish Annotated New Testament*, 2nd ed., ed. Amy-Jill Levine and Marc Zvi Butler. (New York: Oxford University Press, 2017), 35.

spond to the outpouring of God's love, which is the unknown thing. It is the kingdom of God. He uses the known things of the seed and the soil and the agricultural process of planting, growing, and harvesting.

Jesus himself teaches the disciples in Matthew 13:18-23 what this parable means. The seed is the word, Jesus says. Maybe we hear "the word" and think of the gospel of John: "In the beginning was the word …" (John 1:1).

The word is Jesus, John says. Jesus is the word and brings the word, which is the good news of God's love for God's people. The word is not the Bible, but the Bible contains the message of the word, Jesus, God's love—the reason for Jesus: God wanting to bring all people into God's family. Remember this from Abraham and the prophets, that there will be a Messiah who comes to bring together all people into God's family. This seed is that love.

Then Jesus tells us that the path is those who hear the word but don't understand it, so it is snatched by the evil one. He goes on to explain that the rocky soil is those who hear and receive the word but have no root, so they fall away when tested. They like what they hear at first, but when life gets tough, they look to something else.

Jesus then explains that the thorns are those who hear the word, but it gets choked out by the world and love of wealth.

Finally, the good soil is the person who hears the word, receives it, understands it, then bears fruit. Notice that this process that brings good fruit happens intrinsically, naturally, consequently, when the love of God is received and understood. It bears thirty, sixty, a hundredfold—which is an enormous amount. It is hyperbolic, intentionally to surprise and shock the audience. What? Could the word really produce that much? It is beyond imagination.

Notice that out of the four kinds of soil, only one soil takes the seed and yields, and yields such a great amount. The audience would have been astounded that when someone receives and understands—these go together, the receiving and understanding—when this happens, there is the consequent, intrinsic birth of new fruit, fruit that will feed and nourish out of and from the person who receives the word and understands it.

Think about what it means to receive something. We have a role in this kind of interaction. We are open to and accept it, and, therefore, know it in an intimate way. And to understand it, too, means we have grappled with it intellectually, emotionally, and spiritually—something that takes time and energy and effort—and then we end up in a new place of comprehension.

But let's go deeper still and look at the kinds of soil more closely.

KINDS OF SOIL
COMPARISON

What we know (literal, physical)	... compared to	What we don't know (metaphoric, spiritual)
Seed=Source from which life is sustained. This is what God births, literally and physically, to produce food that sustains life. Needs soil, water, light. Grows, gives, produces fruit.		Seed=Word=Jesus=God's love. Also, sustains life, is nourishment, and needs soil (us) to grow.
Soil=Substance, earth, dirt, made by God in which the seed is nourished and can grow		Soil=The hearts of people, our deepest selves, our very souls. The seat of our intellect, reason, emotions.
Path=Worn soil, hard, compacted. Impenetrable. Seed cannot take root, no growth, no fruit. Vulnerable to birds, "evil one" (13:19). Also, a path indicates easiest way, to follow.		Path=We who are rigid, beaten down by people, shallow, weak, dogmatic, proud and therefore do not perceive or understand God's love. Vulnerable to perverting God's word of love, using it in ways God did not intend: sin. Results in pain and suffering, impenetrable to love.
Rocky soil=Something takes up space, gets in the way, no room for roots or seed, rocks are heavy and solid, difficult to remove, requires work, attention, time, energy, blocks growth and nourishment. Results in tiny, weak roots.		Rocky soil=us with sin. Sin (rock) is hard to face, difficult to give up because of fear, weakness, doubt take up space in hearts. Love withers. No fruit. "Endures only for a while" (13:21).
Thorns in soil=Allowed to grow along with seed and takes over. Painful to remove, hurtful, strong, stubborn, requires work, attention, time, energy. Comes back if you don't get the root.		Thorns in soil="The cares of the world and the lure of wealth choke the word" (Matt 13:22), or allowing selfish wants and needs to be stronger than God's love. Love is choked out. No depth, no root.
Good soil=Tilled or upturned. Weeded where we pull up and out. Fed through fertilizers. Watered. Takes time, effort, energy, attention. Roots grow deep, strong, healthy, productive plants grow fruit that gives life and more seed. Also requires knowledge of process: study. Use of intellect.		People who perceive and understand the love of God (13:23) because we have been upturned, repented, confessed, transformed. Fed through knowledge (study) and prayer. Requires willingness, surrender, faith, time, energy, attention. Results in strong vessels of the love of God that is pouring into our hearts. It inherently must go out to the world.

What we know—the literal and physical—is the seed, a small, tiny kernel, the source from which life is sustained, given by God, giving us life. Literally without seed, we have no food, no life. It nourishes us; it is vital. The seed needs soil and water and light. All those together bring the plant that grows and gives fruit and life.

Compare this known seed to what we don't know: the spiritual reality of God's kingdom. What is the seed compared to in God's kingdom? It is the word, Jesus says—God's love. In the same way the literal physical seed feeds our physical selves and gives us life, this word—this message of the gospel, this good news Jesus brings—also sustains our life and nourishes us but in a spiritual way. It, too, is vital. And it needs us to grow. The image is that the seed is planted in us and nourishes us, and then we produce fruit. Then, the love of God goes out into world and feeds others. In the same way, the physical seed turns into food and fruit, the love of God in us gives us life, and then we produce love that gives life to others. So in God's kingdom, then, God's love is planted in every heart and that same love flows out. Imagine how abundant and beautiful if the soil, or we, receive that love.

Let's look then at the soil more closely. Literally what we know is that soil is a substance, tangible, physical, earth and dirt made by God, the place where seed can be nourished. Seed needs soil to feed it and to protect it so it can grow and produce. Like the soil, that's us, our heart, the deepest part of ourselves. It's not the Valentine's Day kind of heart but the very soul. The Greek understanding would have been that the heart is the seat of our intellect, our reason, our emotions, the deepest self.[2] In a metaphoric sense, then, our heart is the soil—this is where the seed grows—and I think this is the difference in listening and not listening. Does the word of God get down into your heart?

Jesus presents four ways that people listen and respond to God's word/love scattered in their hearts. The first is the seed on the path. What kind of soil is this? Let's look at a path, the familiar, tangible reality, the physical thing that we know, and then compare that to the spiritual, metaphoric, intangible reality that we don't know. Literally, the soil on a path is worn down, trodden, beaten down, hard, compacted, and impenetrable. Seed cannot take root here, so no growth happens and no fruit. The seed is exposed and vulnerable, and in the parable, Jesus says it is vulnerable to the evil one. Also, notice, too, that a path indicates the easy way to travel, literally, and many people choose this way.

2. Mark D. Nanos, "The Letter of Paul to the Romans." In *The Jewish Annotated New Testament*, 2nd ed. Edited by Amy-Jill Levine and Marc Zvi Butler. New York: Oxford University Press, 2017.

So who are these people whose hearts are like a worn path? Like a path, they are rigid, dogmatic, beaten down. What we know about a real path is what we know about their heart. It is impenetrable; God's love cannot get into this person's heart. Maybe this heart is someone who has been beaten down by people, worn down, maybe cynical. Also notice that you cannot easily dig into a path. We would need heavy equipment to get the soil on a path turned over or plowed. This heart is the same way: hard-hearted, we call it. Maybe this heart is weak or dogmatic, rigid or proud. This kind of heart is closed up to God's love. Love cannot get in, and so this person is vulnerable to sin. This kind of person is hard, and because God's word of love cannot get into this kind of heart, it results in pain and suffering. We know these people, don't we? They cannot receive love and certainly cannot understand love. Why do you think this is so? Here, Jesus is telling us that some people are not able to hear, listen, receive, or understand the love of God, the good news.

Next is the rocky soil. Here is another kind of heart, another kind of response to the good news of God's love. Let's look at what we know: Literally, the rocks in this soil take up space and get in the way. There is no room for seed, no room for roots to grow because the soil is full of something, and, therefore, the root cannot go deep into the soil. It results in a tiny, shallow root, which makes the plant vulnerable. Also, notice that if you do plant in this soil, the sower would have to get the rocks out. This would require work to remove the heavy rocks, which are solid and hard. This work would be difficult and take time and energy. The rocks block the growth of seed.

The spiritual reality of this heart is that the rocks are the things in our hearts that block us from God, the sins, which are hard for us to face and difficult for us to confront. These sins get in the way of God's love. We have big rocks in our soil that won't allow God's love to get in there. Our initial faith has no depth; there is too much in the way. What are these things? Fear? Maybe fears create a barrier between us and God. Or maybe a weakness or doubt takes up space in our hearts. What else? Many things live in us and come between us and God. And the result is that love withers and no fruit comes from this little plant with such a tiny root. God's love never gets to grow and thrive and produce fruit.

Another kind of soil is one with thorns. Here, the thorns are allowed to grow along with seed. The strong thorns are painful to remove. You have to be strong to get rid of them. They are stubborn. Getting rid of them requires much work, attention, time, and energy. And thorns come back if you don't get the root. So what are these sharp and painful things that we allow to take over instead of God's love? This heart is one where selfish wants and needs are stronger and take over. God's love has no room to grow. What kind of wants and needs? Maybe power or money. "The lure of wealth," Jesus says. Fame or position. And why do we fall victim to the "lure of wealth" and fame? Perhaps it's because we lack the knowledge that we are worthy and valuable and loved by a holy God. Some past pains have left us with a powerful need for value, so money and power become a substitute for God's love, like the thorns. Money and power make us feel more valuable. Is this a choice to allow their hearts to remain full of these strong and powerful thorns, these strong and powerful wants and needs? Do you think that we just ignore the thorns, that we don't want to put in the work to get rid of the thorns?

Then we have the good soil. Good soil literally is the kind that has been fed, worked, tilled, upturned, plowed, and dug into. The rocks have been removed, and the thorns have been grabbed by the roots. This soil is not compacted but upturned, weeded. Literally, the sower knows the soil and has worked to pull things up and out. He/she has given energy and fed and watered, taken time and effort, given it attention. It takes work. In this soil, roots have food and space. They are nourished, and seed can grow and produce fruit. It will do this—it is not a hope. It is definitive. It will produce a plant that will grow fruit. When the seed meets tilled, upturned soil that has been fed and nourished and tended, it will give fruit. The fruit then gives life and more seed. Such a beautiful equation and process!

We are the tree, and the good soil is our hearts where God's love is planted. We who hear God's word of love perceive and understand it. This does not happen immediately. Like a seed, it takes time—maybe a lifetime—to get to a place where the love of God becomes so real to us that we work to upturn our hearts and get the rocks out, to do this work.

We are really talking about repentance here: to recognize that our heart has barriers to God's love, that the rocks are in our hearts and then to confess them and to talk about this reality of our situation and not deny it. To not look at other things but to be attentive to our soil, our hearts. We have been hardened and not receptive. We have not noticed or paid attention to things in the way that come between us and God. When we do, we transform. We become the kind of heart where we grow the love of God, and we grow fruit, and God's love comes through us and we become a tree full of God's love.

How do we feed our soil, our hearts? Till up the hardened dirt, remove the thorns? With study and prayer. This work requires willingness to spend time and energy. It requires surrender in a prayer: God, show me the rocks, the thorns. This prayer requires faith that God can do this. Jesus says God will do this—it's definitive. It requires your time, that you give of yourself and your energy. You will need to take energy from something else that is not feeding you and put that energy toward this prayer and study. You will need to practice recognizing God's presence. We can be good soil where the word of God's love can grow us into strong trees with deep roots. We are the yielders of God's love that must go out to world. And, like the tree that grows fruit, it happens intrinsically.

Let's look at the fruit. Literally, physically, we can imagine an apple that feeds and nourishes. We can imagine orchards and orchards full of apples waiting to be picked and eaten. Imagine the love of God the same way, where it is available for and goes out to feed and nourish the world—out to our children, to everyone—from us, the good soil. If our hearts are ready.

What kind of soil are you? Ponder this: Are we good soil who hear and understand and bear fruit and yield beyond our comprehension? What kind of soil do we want to be—can we be good soil? Yes, Jesus says. It takes work, though.

One way to turn us into good soil can be found in *Opening to God* by David Benner. Benner claims that our willingness and our attention to God will change us and turn us into "good soil." Benner says that contemplative prayer "removes the blocks to openness to God … that obstruct the channels of our self that need to be open if we are to experience the fullness of the life of God … our signature sins."[3] Our signature sins are the things that obstruct us, like the beaten path, the rock, the thorns. All of these are obstructions that keep us from God and love.

Hear that!

Benner goes on to clarify what those sins or rocks and thorns are: "addictions, anxieties, unresolved conflicts, unhealed traumatic experiences, wounds and fears."[4] These are just a few. Sit in that thought for a minute.

There are things in our hearts that keep us from God, and maybe we don't even know they are there. They may be boulders, not just rocks. Pains people have done to us that we all have that go back years and years and still have a place in our hearts. Or maybe we do not even know what these things are that we want to remove—and it is not easy to upturn soil.

But Benner implores us to "[t]urn to God with whatever mea-

3. David Benner, *Opening to God: Lectio Divina and Life as Prayer*, expanded ed. (Downer's Grove: InterVarsity Press, 2021), 169.
4. Benner, *Opening to God*, 169.

sure of trust we have and allow God's life to flow into ours. As we do so, divine love reveals the obstacles ... and if we are willing to release [them] ... they are transformed ... into the likeness of Christ."[5] Divine love reveals those rocks in us and transforms them.

So what are we waiting for? This is the calling on us, but some are not going to hear what Jesus says, and here's why: the stuff in our soil/heart. But it is not impossible. God will transform them. It's not "if" God will, but absolutely, definitively, we "can" heal those—God can do it. Remember what we have to do, which is to turn to God with whatever measure of trust we have and allow God's love to flow into our heart.

Just do this: Pray for God to reveal those rocks and thorns and paths. Say: I'm going to be willing to release those things. And if we do, we become big, giant, beautiful, strong trees that yield enormous amounts. It is beyond our comprehension how much love we could release into this world.

This is what God is trying to do. This is what God wants to do. This is repentance, confession, and God's love poured into our upturned hearts.

If this transformation happens, then what we waiting for? Ask yourself:
- What kind of soil am I?
- What is my soil/my heart full of?
- Am I looking at things other than God?
- What kind of soil do I want to be?

Remember, we started and ended this parable with the word "listen." Are we listening? Are we comprehending this enormous love of God poured into the world through Jesus?

We could, then, say this parable is telling us that the kingdom of God grows and brings love to feed the world's hearts when the hearts of people are fed and nourished by God, when the people's hearts are cleared of all things/sins that are barriers between them and God, when the people have given themselves to God through a willingness to study and pray and look at those sins and thorns and hardness. The whole landscape will change. God's love will come up through these strong roots and healthy trees and go out into the world.

Step Three: Final questions
What else do you see, observe, notice?
What was the loudest, most thought-provoking thing for you over this

---

5. Benner, *Opening to God*, 172-73.

week of study?

What do you think and feel God is saying to you through this parable?

Does this insight move your heart toward some kind of repentance and renewal?

Chapter Two
The Parable of the Wedding Banquet/ Great Dinner

Matthew 22:1-10; Luke 14:15-24

Step One: Follow the "Read and Study" plan for the week:

Monday: Pray for an open, listening heart. Then, in expectation, read the parable at least once. Close the Bible and sit quietly in contemplation of what you just read. Maybe draw a picture or sketch of the parable during this quiet contemplation. Or maybe search images of the parable. But only search images, no commentaries, etc.

Tuesday: Pray for an open, listening heart. Again, in expectation, read the parable at least once, maybe out loud. If the parable appears in more than one gospel, read each version. Pay attention to the differences and similarities. Underline or highlight what you notice. Do these differences alter the parable? Write down your answer. What do you think is being compared? What do your Bible footnotes say about the parable? Does this information add to your thoughts on the parable? Sit quietly in contemplation of this exercise.

Wednesday: Begin with prayer and expectation. Read the parable. Today, notice what action precedes the parable. Is this information helpful? In what way? Now, notice the action that follows the parable. Is this action tied to the parable in any way? Does the location of the parable impact your understanding? Do you see it in a new way, or does it alter the meaning at all? Is the location the same in each version? How are they different? Then, sit quietly in contemplation of this exercise.

Thursday: As always, begin with the prayer for an open, listening heart. In expectation, read the parable. Let's look at the characters. Who are they? Notice what each character says. What do they do? Can you identify the motives for their actions? Why do you think they do what they do and say what they say? What else do you notice about each character? Now, look at the setting of the parable. Where does the action take place? Why do you think Jesus uses this setting? The commentary in your study Bible may help. Next, where do you notice conflict or tension? Now, sit quietly in contemplation.

Friday: Begin with prayer, as usual. Read the parable. Look back over your notes from the week. What do you hear after this week's study? What is this parable teaching you? Some things to consider: Which character do you seem to focus on the most? Can you answer why? What does this parable tell you about who God is? What does this parable tell you about what matters to God? What does this parable tell you about how God's kingdom operates? Sit in quiet contemplation of these questions. Maybe draw a picture or write down a word that seems to speak to you. What is God revealing to you?

Saturday: After your prayer of expectation and surrender, and after having spent the week reading, thinking, praying, and listening to this parable, read the following discussion. Perhaps you will gain more clarity or affirmation, or maybe something else will arise for you. Write down your thoughts, observations, questions, and concerns. Finally, what do you feel that God is revealing to you in this parable?

Sunday: Rest and pray in quiet contemplation of the parable.

Step Two: Discussion

The main question that most interested me after comparing these two versions of the parable in Matthew and Luke was: Why are they different? So, let's first note the differences (see table, next page).

First, notice the bold text areas in each column of the table. Matthew has Jesus teaching this parable to the disciples, while Luke presents the parable as Jesus's response to a guest at a wedding dinner. Matthew has a king invite guests, yet Luke has "someone" give the dinner. In both versions, slaves[1] are

---

1. This word "slave" rightly has a serious negative connotation for our modern culture. In this parable, I hope that it is clear that Jesus is taking a known part of the Roman culture in which he and his audience live in order to compare roles in an entirely figurative way. In no way does this role in this parable justify slavery. Slavery was a part of the lives of the Roman economic and societal system; that is why Jesus uses it. Jesus is not in any way condoning slavery and neither am I in using it in this study. For a comprehensive explanation of Roman society and the role of slavery, read *Slavery in the Roman Empire* by R. H. Barrow (London: Methuen, 2022) or *The Roman Empire: Economy, Society, and Culture* by Peter Garnsey and Richard Saller (Berkeley: University of California Press, 2015).

MATTHEW VS. LUKE
A COMPARISON

Matthew 22:1-10 (NRSV)
The Parable of the Wedding Banquet

Luke 14:15-25 (NRSV)
The Parable of the Great Dinner

Once more Jesus spoke to them in parables, saying: The kingdom of heaven may be compared to a king who gave a wedding banquet for his son. He sent his slaves to call those who had been invited to the wedding banquet, but they would not come. Again he sent other slaves, saying, 'Tell those who have been invited: Look, I have prepared my dinner, my oxen and my fat calves have been slaughtered, and everything is ready; come to the wedding banquet.' But they made light of it and went away, one to his farm, another to his business, *while the rest seized his slaves, mistreated them, and killed them. The king was enraged. He sent his troops, destroyed those murderers, and burned their city.* Then he said to his slaves, 'The wedding is ready, but those invited were not worthy. Go therefore into the main streets, and invite everyone you find to the wedding banquet.' Those slaves went out into the streets and gathered all whom they found, both good and bad; so the wedding hall was filled with guests.

One of the dinner guests, on hearing this, said to him, "Blessed is anyone who will eat bread in the kingdom of God!" Then Jesus said to him, "Someone gave a great dinner and invited many. At the time for the dinner he sent his slave to say to those who had been invited, 'Come; for everything is ready now.' But they all alike began to make excuses. The first said to him, 'I have bought a piece of land, and I must go out and see it; please accept my regrets.' Another said, 'I have bought five yoke of oxen, and I am going to try them out; please accept my regrets.' Another said, 'I have just been married, and therefore I cannot come.' So the slave returned and reported this to his master. *Then the owner of the house became angry* and said to his slave, 'Go out at once into the streets and lanes of the town and bring in the poor, the crippled, the blind, and the lame.' And the slave said, 'Sir, what you ordered has been done, and there is still room.' Then the master said to the slave, 'Go out into the roads and lanes, and compel people to come in, so that my house may be filled. For I tell you, none of those who were invited will taste my dinner.'"

sent to invite guests to the event.

Next, consider the underlined text areas in the table. These show the differences between the responses of those who were invited to the banquet/dinner. In Matthew, the invitees "make light of" the king's invitation and simply go away back to their daily lives. Luke, however, tells us that the guests "made excuses." They go take on other tasks, importantly, that are trivial, which would have insulted the host.

Finally, the italicized text areas in the table show us the differences in how those slaves who brought the invitations were treated by the invitees. In Matthew, the invitees kill the slaves; not so in Luke. Also, in Matthew, the "king was enraged" at the murder of his slaves, and so, dramatically, the king sends troops to kill the invitees and burn their city, while Luke's host simply becomes angry. No murderous king in Luke's version. But Matthew's murderous king also notes that as the banquet is ready, the invitees are "not worthy" and now sends the slaves to invite "everyone." Luke's version has the host send slaves to invite specific people: "poor, crippled, blind, and lame." Then, the host "compels" everyone to come to the ready feast. It is here at the end of the story that Luke's host says that none of those invited will get to eat.

Do these differences matter? Yes, especially if and when we only read one version. If we only read Matthew's version, we may focus on the king who is a murderer. This violent image can be confusing. Is the king supposed to be God? Why does Luke change the parable? Or maybe Luke doesn't change it; maybe Matthew puts it in. After all, a parable compares the known to the unknown, and we know kings. Isn't Jesus using a king to teach us about God and God's kingdom? Why not a king and a murder in Luke? Does Luke change the parable? Why? Or does Matthew change it? Does it matter?

If we look at the historical context of the gospels, we can come to some clarity. Matthew and Luke were both written after the destruction of the second temple in AD 70. Both writers lived through this violent, deadly time. To them and the Jewish world, the temple was the place where God touched earth, where humans could encounter God, a holy space and place. So for the Romans to destroy this holy place was both devastating and significant. This context is important in understanding the differences in the two gospel versions.

It seems Matthew writes his gospel with this horrific event undergirding his gospel.[2]

---

2. Warren Carter, "The Gospel According to Matthew" in *The New Interpreter's Study Bible* (Nashville: Abingdon, 2003), 1786.

He sees the destruction of the temple as God's punishment on the Jewish people for rejecting Jesus, according to scholars. Therefore, he boldly and blatantly writes the parable with a king who acts the same way: the king behaves like the Romans. What the king does in the parable is what the Romans did to Jerusalem. Think of it this way. God has the banquet ready for Israel and has sent his son to invite Israel. But Israel has "made light" of the invitation. God responds dramatically.

But Luke is different. He writes his gospel later than Matthew. Furthermore, scholars note that Luke's parable is in a different location in his gospel: it falls after Jesus dining with a Pharisee where he focuses on humility (don't take the best seat at the table), then Jesus tells this story where the focus is on inviting those who cannot reciprocate. Romans only invited those who could benefit them politically, and the culture demanded that you must reciprocate an invitation. Invitations were not based on relationship or friendship but rather on obligation. The motive was always selfish, and Jesus confronts this ideology. Scholars think Luke puts this parable here as an example of "someone who gave a dinner" and did so for "the poor, the lame, the blind" because they cannot reciprocate—so then the parable serves as a model for humility and selflessness. Inviting such guests demonstrates a different kind of heart and functions as a stark and shocking contrast to the Roman world. So in Luke's story, Jesus teaches that such inclusive behavior is the way the kingdom of God operates; inclusion and generosity are attributes of God's. God invites people—there is no reciprocation necessary—and rejoices in a great celebration when they accept the invitation.

So what is important in noting these differences? Where do we really need to focus? Maybe we need to look at the similarities and try to discern what Jesus is teaching about God and God's kingdom. What spiritual truth is he teaching with this parable/comparison? What is Jesus telling us about God? Let's go back and look at the elements of the story and dig down into the message as we remember that parables are comparisons between the known and the unknown. Parables take a real-life situation and use it to show something about God's kingdom.

The characters in both versions are the king/host, the son (in Matthew), slaves, invited guests, everyone in the street, the poor, and we have the event itself. The king/host literally is the one throwing the event, who owns the kingdom, the one in power, the authority, who issues the invitation, and finally opens the event up to everyone, including those who can't reciprocate.

Everyone except those who did not take the invitation seriously. Or maybe they ignored it.

Who is this earthly king compared to? Scholars agree that this king/host is God. We can see that God invites everyone, even the Gentiles, even those who we humans think are not worthy. We also note that God responds to those who reject the invitation. In Matthew, it's a violent response. In Luke, God is angry. Anger is in both versions. Think about what this emotion says about God. Anger is evoked by hurt. Can we see that Jesus is teaching us that God hurts when humans reject God? Pain from rejection only occurs if love is present. Clearly, we see God reaching out in expectation and in love to relationship with humanity, and then responding as one who has been hurt and rejected by the beloved. Don't they want to come celebrate the son giving himself in covenant? God seems to desire human response to this truth. What happens to God's pain? We also see that humans have a choice to accept this invitation to relationship, and some don't. We also see God as generous and vulnerable, even. Extravagant and inclusive. The only ones left out are those who choose not to attend.

And what is the event that we are invited to? This idea of a feast or banquet or dinner is coming from the Old Testament, from the prophets, from Isaiah and Hosea. Jesus is using this image from the Old Testament to teach us something. This banquet could be teaching us about the Eschaton, or the Second Coming, and according to this parable, all are invited, including Israel. And this event is a marriage of the Son, Jesus. A covenantal relationship is being celebrated. The king is giving this event to celebrate his son's giving of himself in covenantal relationship. Or it could be the kingdom come, where all things are new and will operate as God desires. Or perhaps it is the kingdom here on earth, life here as God desires, treating people as God does.

Imagine that banquet, with the table set, glasses and china, music, lights, laughter, friends, family, love, dancing, delicious food ready and waiting, prepared for you. For all people. We might also imagine this feast as the Lord's Supper, the Eucharist, Holy Communion; happening now in this moment. We are invited to come and receive this means of grace in this sacrament, now. It is not something we need to wait for; it is present now. It is a way God joins with us and feeds us spiritually with the real presence of Christ. God's presence is here among us, the reality of God's love incarnate in Jesus. We say so in our communion liturgy. We say that this table is open. It is ready. We are invited to come feast—not just on good food, but on this spiritual reality of God's love incarnate in Jesus.

So both a present feast and a future feast. Either way, what does this parable teach us about that event? Or time, or place, or life? It is life with God in this world now, and it will be life with God in the future. And that life is abundant love and joy prepared for all people.

Some observations/conclusions:
- A feast = a dinner
- Food = life
- Nurture, made strong
- Pleasure
- Joy
- Celebration
- Relationships
- Connections
- Laughter
- Beauty
- Abundance/plenty
- Covenant, like a wedding
- Celebrate the relationship of love, like a wedding

God is the inviter, the preparer. And who is going to this event? According to Jesus, what does this say about God?
- God gives, no reciprocation necessary, free
- God prepares life and nurture for us
- God wants the best for us—the guests, the invited who accept the invitation
- Gives in abundance, more than we need or imagine
- Cares
- Loves
- Knows us, invites us
- Celebrates extravagantly our acceptance and attendance, all for us.
- Are we going to accept the invitation?

This parable, we can say, is really about grace. God is inviting us to the kind of life God desires. Like John Wesley's idea of prevenient grace, the invitation is always open and calling us toward God. Jesus is the Son—a joining with us in a spiritual covenant.

And God will celebrate our acceptance and attendance. With more than we can imagine: joy and peace and love and life.

Come to the banquet. We can trust this—hope and certainty, eternal and absolute. Now and in the future, the not yet/already. The banquet is life with God.

Step Three: Final Questions

What else do you see, observe, notice?

What was the loudest, most thought-provoking thing for you over this week of study?

What do you think and feel God is saying to you through this parable?

Does this insight move your heart toward some kind of repentance and renewal?

Chapter Three
The Parable of the Tenants

Matthew 21:33-46; Mark 12:1-12; Luke 20:9-19

Step One: Follow the "Read and Study" plan for the week:

Monday: Pray for an open, listening heart. Then, in expectation, read the parable at least once. Close the Bible and sit quietly in contemplation of what you just read. Maybe draw a picture or sketch of the parable during this quiet contemplation. Or maybe search images of the parable. But only search images, no commentaries, etc.

Tuesday: Pray for an open, listening heart. Again, in expectation, read the parable at least once, maybe out loud. If the parable appears in more than one gospel, read each version. Pay attention to the differences and similarities. Underline or highlight what you notice. Do these differences alter the parable? Write down your answer. What do you think is being compared? What do your Bible footnotes say about the parable? Does this information add to your thoughts on the parable? Sit quietly in contemplation of this exercise.

Wednesday: Begin with prayer and expectation. Read the parable. Today, notice what action precedes the parable. Is this information helpful? In what way? Now, notice the action that follows the parable. Is this action tied to the parable in any way? Does the location of the parable impact your understanding? Do you see it in a new way, or does it alter the meaning at all? Is the location the same in each version? How are they different? Then, sit quietly in contemplation of this exercise.

Thursday: As always, begin with the prayer for an open, listening heart. In expectation, read the parable. Let's look at the characters. Who are they? Notice what each character says. What do they do? Can you identify the motives

19

for their actions? Why do you think they do what they do and say what they say? What else do you notice about each character? Now, look at the setting of the parable. Where does the action take place? Why do you think Jesus uses this setting? The commentary in your study Bible may help. Next, where do you notice conflict or tension? Now, sit quietly in contemplation.

Friday: Begin with prayer, as usual. Read the parable. Look back over your notes from the week. What do you hear after this week's study? What is this parable teaching you? Some things to consider: Which character do you seem to focus on the most? Can you answer why? What does this parable tell you about who God is? What does this parable tell you about what matters to God? What does this parable tell you about how God's kingdom operates? Sit in quiet contemplation of these questions. Maybe draw a picture or write down a word that seems to speak to you. What is God revealing to you?

Saturday: After your prayer of expectation and surrender, and after having spent the week reading, thinking, praying, and listening to this parable, read the following discussion. Perhaps you will gain more clarity or affirmation, or maybe something else will arise for you. Write down your thoughts, observations, questions, and concerns. Finally, what do you feel God is revealing?

Sunday: Rest and pray in quiet contemplation of the parable.

Step Two: Discussion

The Parable of the Wicked Tenants is in all three gospels. Therefore, we can say that it was important to the gospel writers, and so this makes us want to give more time to discerning the message.

We have read this parable throughout the week, and perhaps we have drawn a picture of something like this:

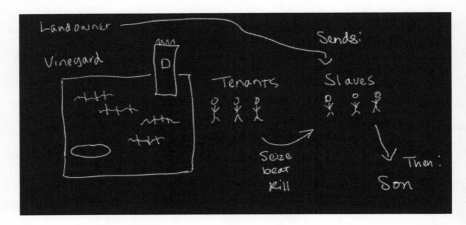

So let's summarize the parable first, which by now is very familiar. We have the landowner who plants a vineyard with a watchtower and a wine press and a fence around it. He leases it to tenants and then sends slaves to get the harvest. But the tenants seize, beat, and kill the slaves, so finally the landowner says he will send his son, thinking that they will surely respect his son. But they don't; they throw him out of vineyard and kill him. Jesus then asks his audience what the landowner would do. They all say that he would kill the tenants and put someone else in charge. As Jesus continues, we hear that that's what the landowner did. Then, we have the second part of parable, where Jesus says the stone the builders have rejected has become the cornerstone or the keystone, which is the highest stone at the top of a curved architectural feature in a building. This stone literally holds everything up, and without this stone, it would fall.

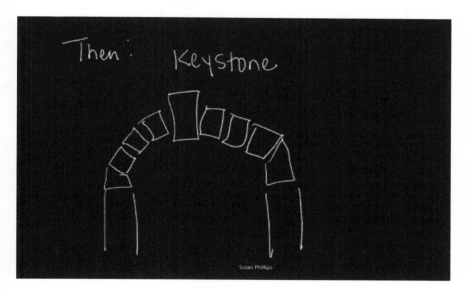

Suzan Phillips

Let's look now at the context. It is important to see where the parable is located within the story. First, we notice that Jesus is in Jerusalem and it is Holy Week, the time when Jesus is getting ready to be crucified. He has just come to Jerusalem and just had the Palm Sunday event, and now he is in the temple as he tells this parable. He has been teaching the people there with the temple leaders present. And he has just cleansed temple because he was upset that people were having to pay for sacrificial animals (remember that sacrificing gave them forgiveness of their sins). He says that God's house has become a "den of robbers," a phrase from Jeremiah, which would have been known and easily recognized by the audience, and now the leaders have just asked Jesus, "By what authority are you doing these things, and who gave you this authority?" (Matthew 21:23 NRSV). They ask Jesus this question because they were the authorities. They knew the law and told the people what God wanted and the life God wanted.

So the question for the people standing there becomes: Who is it that speaks for God? Who do we listen to? Is it the leaders we have always listened to? Or this new teacher? A question hangs in the air and creates the tension in this scene. Who speaks for God? To answer this question, Jesus tells this parable.

Let's remember the significance of this location, too. The temple is where God is located and where God interacts with humans. It holds great significance for the people, and here is Jesus, here in this place, teaching, while the temple leaders stand and watch! Surely all who were present were on edge.

We have said throughout this study that parable are comparisons. So, what kind of comparison is this parable? According to scholars, it is an allegory.[1]

You may remember from the introduction that, according to the Oxford Concise Dictionary of the Christian Church, an allegory "speak[s] one thing and signifies something other than what is said."[2]

Using allegories to teach was a traditional way of interpreting the Torah; it was a clever way to talk about something so that the audience would have to think and wrestle with the lesson. Let's look, then, at this parable allegorically, a comparison that uses something they know to show something they don't know.

Remember, Jesus is answering the question: Who has authority to teach about God? So it's like Jesus says: You know this? Well, this other thing is just like that. And the result is that we understand. In order to more clearly understand Jesus, we need to look closely at the elements of the story and seek to identify what they signify.

The first element of the parable is the vineyard. Why a vineyard? If we are not familiar with the Old Testament, as the audience would have been, we may miss that the vineyard is Israel, God's chosen people. In fact, this image comes directly from Isaiah 5:1-7.

1. Mary Ann Tolbert, "The Gospel According to Mark" in *The New Interpreter's Study Bible*, Walter Harrelson (Nashville: Abingdon, 2003), 1832.

2. E. A. Livingstone, ed. *The Oxford Concise Dictionary of the Christian Church*, third edition. (Oxford: Oxford University Press, 2013), 15.

Isaiah 5:1-7 (NRSVA)
The Song of the Unfruitful Vineyard

1 Let me sing for my beloved my love-song concerning his vineyard:
My beloved had a vineyard on a very fertile hill.
2 He dug it and cleared it of stones, and planted it with choice vines;
he built a watch-tower in the midst of it, and hewed out a wine vat in it;
he expected it to yield grapes, but it yielded wild grapes.
3 And now, inhabitants of Jerusalem and people of Judah,
judge between me and my vineyard.
4 What more was there to do for my vineyard that I have not done in it?
When I expected it to yield grapes, why did it yield wild grapes?
5 And now I will tell you what I will do to my vineyard.
I will remove its hedge, and it shall be devoured;
I will break down its wall, and it shall be trampled down.
6 I will make it a waste; it shall not be pruned or hoed,
and it shall be overgrown with briers and thorns;
I will also command the clouds that they rain no rain upon it.
7 For the vineyard of the Lord of hosts is the house of Israel,
and the people of Judah are his pleasant planting;
he expected justice, but saw bloodshed;
righteousness, but heard a cry!

The minute Jesus says, "A landowner who has a vineyard," the audience would have immediately connected what Jesus is saying to the fifth chapter of Isaiah because this image came from their scriptures that they knew well. They also would have understood the context of Isaiah. See how complicated the context gets? Knowing the context adds richness to our understanding and to the beauty of scripture. We have Jesus and his context, but we also have Isaiah and his context to understand and unpack. The leaders would also know Isaiah's context, too, of course. Here is Jesus, in between the temple leaders and the people, referring to Isaiah and challenging those leaders, all while the people are listening, observing, and watching this conflict. The people are waiting to see what Jesus will say to these leaders who have been teaching and leading them.

Now, Isaiah was a prophet, and recall what the prophets were doing: calling out Israel for their rotten fruit. They were saying: You, Israel, have been God's people, but now you are unfaithful, and your fruit is now rotten. It is "wild" or noxious, rotten. But, these prophets continue to Israel, God will send a messiah to save you. This was the prophets' message.

Let's look closely at Isaiah and focus on verse 5. This is Israel speaking here, and notice this language is identical to the parable: wild grapes or noxious grapes. This voice we hear speaking is Israel's voice and God is the "beloved." That is how Isaiah speaks of the relationship between Israel and God; it is like a marriage. We hear the same language in Isaiah as in the parable, with the vineyard, vines, tower, and vat. And therefore, it is clear to the audience that Jesus is using Isaiah. They know that Israel is God's vineyard that God himself plants.

Look now at verse 7. It is Israel who are the people of God and his pleasant planting. God plants these people in the world to bring about the kind of life he wants in the world. He plants them there; they are choice vines. God plants the house of Israel. But now Isaiah is telling Israel that God "expected justice (in his vineyard) but got blood, expected righteousness but heard a cry." Their fruit is noxious and rotten. Israel is not bringing the kind of life God wants in the world.

Next we have the elements of the landowner and the grapes. God, as the landowner, plants the life-giving produce, the vines, and then leases his vineyard to Israel so they will take care of it. These literal parts tell us God provides what is necessary for their lives—food and drink—and he surrounds and protects them. Perhaps the grapes signify the Law. The Law is the prescription for them to be able to be holy. God not only provides for their physical well-being and life but also provides a way for them to be holy: be obedient to the law, which leads to life as God envisions it. Through God's actions, we can see that God loves and trusts his people.

The next element is the tenants, those given authority and responsibility to care for God's people and lead them to obedience. Clearly, the tenants signify the temple leaders who seize, beat, stone, kill, and go for the son's inheritance. What do these actions tell us about the temple leaders? Jesus is saying that the leaders are the same as these tenants—greedy and violent—and he is saying this in front of those leaders and the people! He claims that the leaders cause problems between Israel and God by perverting the Law. This description of the leaders' violent and selfish behavior is like Rome. We also see this same behavior revealed in the money changers. Such perversion of the Law is exactly what Isaiah is talking about with Israel. Jesus, then, calls that forward by saying things now are the same as when Isaiah told his prophecy.

The next element is the slaves, who are sent by the landowner to collect the harvest. So who are these people? They are the prophets like Jeremiah, Isaiah, and Daniel, whom God sent to his people Israel, those who are charged to take care of God's vineyard. Like the prophets, these slaves are thrown out of the vineyard, dismissed.

Then the landowner, or God, sends his "beloved son" (Luke 20:13). Where have we heard this phrase? We heard it at Jesus's baptism, and now we hear it again here: a connection the audience and gospel writers would surely catch. This "beloved son" would be Jesus. It was not cryptic. And, it also points back to the Old Testament when Abraham is going to sacrifice his beloved son Isaac. All of this would have been recalled and known by the audience.

Allegorically, then, the tenants throw the son out of the father's vineyard and kill him, and what is this telling us? What does this signify? That the temple leaders are going to throw Jesus out and kill him, and we know that this is what happens. This is Jesus predicting his death again.

Jesus asks the people how they think the landowner will respond. They say the landowner will seize them and kill them and lease his vineyard to others who will give him his fruit. We can see this is really that God will give authority over the vineyard to others and speak through others who will lead his people to a life that will manifest God's kingdom/love. When the leaders hear this part of the parable, they reply, "heaven forbid" (Luke 20:17). We must understand that Jesus is saying here that the temple will be given to other leaders—right in front of the current leaders and the people!

Finally, Jesus uses Psalm 118:22-23: "The stone that has been rejected has become the keystone." Let's look at Psalm 118:26-27: "Blessed is he who comes in the name of the Lord. From the house of the Lord we bless you. The Lord is God, and he has made his light shine on us. With boughs in hand, join in the festal procession up to the horns of the altar" (NIV).

We see the phrase here that the crowds just shouted at Jesus as he came into Jerusalem a few days earlier on Palm Sunday. Once again, this is not cryptic to the audience there nor to the leaders who both know this psalm and the events of the last few days. They would certainly make the connection to Jesus. So is what Jesus saying?

It's about the keystone.

God places the rejected stone, Jesus, as the keystone, who brings everything together and gives strength to God's temple. This is not a literal temple but a spiritual one, a spiritual center.

Jesus is rejected and killed, but then becomes the keystone, at the highest point, exalted, resurrected, raised up, and holds everything together.

Two important things to note in this parable/allegory: God's people being turned over to someone else right there in the temple as Jesus speaks and teaches; then, Jesus becomes the center of the spiritual temple without which the entire thing falls down.

Step Three: Final Questions

What else do you see, observe, notice?

What was the loudest, most thought-provoking thing for you over this week of study?

What do you think and feel God is saying to you through this parable?

Does this insight move your heart toward some kind of repentance and renewal?

Chapter Four
The Parable of the Lost Son

Luke 15:11-32

Step One: Follow the "Read and Study" plan for the week:

Monday: Pray for an open, listening heart. Then, in expectation, read the parable at least once. Close the Bible and sit quietly in contemplation of what you just read. Maybe draw a picture or sketch of the parable during this quiet contemplation. Or maybe search images of the parable. But only search images, no commentaries, etc.

Tuesday: Pray for an open, listening heart. Again, in expectation, read the parable at least once, maybe out loud. If the parable appears in more than one gospel, read each version. Pay attention to the differences and similarities. Underline or highlight what you notice. Do these differences alter the parable? Write down your answer. What do you think is being compared? What do your Bible footnotes say about the parable? Does this information add to your thoughts on the parable? Sit quietly in contemplation of this exercise.

Wednesday: Begin with prayer and expectation. Read the parable. Today, notice what action precedes the parable. Is this information helpful? In what way? Now, notice the action that follows the parable. Is this action tied to the parable in any way? Does the location of the parable impact your understanding? Do you see it in a new way, or does it alter the meaning at all? Is the location the same in each version? How are they different? Then, sit quietly in contemplation of this exercise.

Thursday: As always, begin with the prayer for an open, listening heart. In expectation, read the parable. Let's look at the characters. Who are they?

Notice what each character says. What do they do? Can you identify the motives for their actions? Why do you think they do what they do and say what they say? What else do you notice about each character? Now, look at the setting of the parable. Where does the action take place? Why do you think Jesus uses this setting? The commentary in your study Bible may help. Next, where do you notice conflict or tension? Now, sit quietly in contemplation of this exercise.

Friday: Begin with prayer, as usual. Read the parable. Look back over your notes from the week. What do you hear after this week's study? What is this parable teaching you? Some things to consider: Which character do you seem to focus on the most? Can you answer why? What does this parable tell you about who God is? What does this parable tell you about what matters to God? What does this parable tell you about how God's kingdom operates? Sit in quiet contemplation of these questions. Maybe draw a picture or write down a word that seems to speak to you. What is God revealing to you?

Saturday: After your prayer of expectation and surrender, and after having spent the week reading, thinking, praying, and listening to this parable, read the following discussion. Perhaps you will gain more clarity or affirmation, or maybe something else will arise for you. Write down your thoughts, observations, questions, and concerns. Finally, what do you feel that God is revealing to you in this parable?

Sunday: Rest and pray in quiet contemplation of the parable.

Step Two: Discussion

The Prodigal Son—we know the story very well. We've heard it taught and preached plenty of times. Maybe through this week of reading closely and this discussion, we have heard something new.

This is the third of three lost and found parables. The lost sheep and the lost coin come right before this parable, which is only found in Luke. Contextually, just before these parables, Jesus has been asked by the Pharisees what kind of teacher he is because he eats with tax collectors and sinners. Jesus tells these parables to answer this question.

The parable begins with "a man had two sons" (Luke 15:11). Scholar and theologian Amy-Jill Levine says that this phrase would have made the audience think of Old Testament stories like Cain and Abel, or Jacob and Esau.[1]

---

1. Amy-Jill Levine, *Short Stories by Jesus: The Enigmatic Parables of a Controversial Rabbi* (New York: Harper One, 2014), 50.

It brings to mind immediately sibling rivalry, so the audience would think that they know then how this story will turn out: conflict, which could be why one would start the story with this phrase, to recall those stories. Joseph and his brothers is another story that they would remember. Immediately upon hearing this phrase, "a man had two sons," then, sets up the idea of sibling rivalry and conflict and intentionally so, it seems.

First, let's look at the characters. Let's begin with the younger son and walk through what the younger son says. "Give me my property," he says, and then he leaves and squanders all of it in dissolute living. What kind of son is this? What do we think of this? Levine says that he is an "irresponsible, self-indulgent, and probably indulged child"[2] that he would ask for his inheritance this way. Notice, too, that the father says "Okay." We may ask, why does this son want to leave? He ends up in a famine and penniless in a place that blatantly reveals to the audience that he is not in Jewish land because even archeological evidence shows there were no pigs in Jewish communities. He has gone far from home, and now he is in need. But as a foreigner, he gets no help from anyone and no one gives him anything. This state he finds himself in contrasts starkly to his state at the beginning; here no one gives him anything, but at home with his father, he is given everything. He is "lost," a word that connotes no hope and no salvation.

Then he came to himself. We see here a turn, a change, a shift, the kind of language that indicates something has changed in his heart. He determines to go to his father and say, "I have sinned and am no longer worthy to be called son." Is he repentant? Is that why he is going home? Levine doesn't think so. She believes that he is insincere or manipulative.[3] The audience would have thought that he had some sort of conversion because in their mind, coming to himself would indicate a return to God. He acknowledges that he has lost his identity and honor as a son and is no longer worthy to be called son. These words in the mouth of the prodigal son would have made the audience think of a sinner before God and leads us to see that this father most likely represents God.

Now let's look closely at the father. He gives his property and divides it between the two sons, which was unusual because the older would have been entitled to two-thirds, but it seems that the father gives the younger son an equal amount.[4] He does not ask the son why he wants his inheritance now. Is

---

2. Levine, *Short Stories by Jesus*, 51.
3. Levine, *Short Stories by Jesus*, 58.
4. Levine, *Short Stories by Jesus*, 53.

he a weak father, or is he a generous father? We also see an emotional father. While his son is still far off, his father sees him and is filled with compassion. He even seems to be waiting on him to come back, and then he runs out and puts arms around him and kisses him. We see such an emotional response here. Such compassion is a gut response, a heart response, an immediate and deeply emotional response to something that hits you in gut. The word used here—compassion—is the same word used in the Good Samaritan, and it means that it is such a deep emotion that you must respond, and you do so immediately, without thinking.

So, then, we can see how the father feels. He is overcome. Even before the son speaks, the father shows a physical expression of love, an overwhelming response that can only come from love. Notice that the father does not even acknowledge his son's words but immediately calls the slave and asks for the robe, the ring, the sandals, and the fatted calf. A fatted calf was only killed for extremely special occasions, so this gesture indicates the importance of this celebration for the father. He says that this son of mine was dead but now is alive; he was lost and now is found. Two extremes, dead and lost go together and alive and found go together, not literally but spiritually. The ring would recall Joseph receiving a ring from Pharaoh. Rings bestow power and position, and the audience immediately would see that the father is restoring this lost son. Sandals were given when taking possession of land, so here they symbolize the lost son's restoration; he is again a landowner, a part of the family. The sandals are significant to mention here because no one wore sandals in the home and to give them again indicates that the son is restored. The father restores the son yet doesn't even acknowledge the son's sin or shame. Is this how we expect a father to behave? Is this how we expect God to behave?

Which character pricks our hearts? Is it the older son? He is in the field and hears music. This is how he learns something is going on. The slave knows what is happening and says, "Your brother has come ... your father ..." highlighting the family connection. The older son's response is anger to this news. Then the father responds to him just as he responded with the younger son; the father comes to him in the field and pleads with him. Why does the older son not know? When the slaves says the younger brother is "saved," this word would call to mind "salvation" for the audience. Can you hear a spiritual truth underneath the story? It's using something we know to tell us something about God. The younger son is saved, and the older son is angry about it. We see this kind of reaction in other parables like the hired workers.

The righteous become jealous of the sinner who receives mercy. This older son has been dutiful, submissive, and faithful, and he is bitter and jealous and left out.

What does this tell us about God and us? Should the older son feel this way? Do we expect this kind of response? Does it resonate with us? The older son says to the father, "Listen, I have done all the right things but you never even gave me a goat. That son of yours 'came back.'" He then names the younger son's sin, which were extreme things and highly insulting to the father. He devoured your property, he says. See the contrast between the sons? The older son won't even call the younger son "brother." We see disparities between the two sons. Was the father weak? Is the younger son spoiled? But notice that the father does go to this older son the same way he went out to the younger son. Is this how families work? Was the older treated unfairly? What is the older feeling? Is he right? Do we connect with him?

Look at the father with the older son: the father calls him "son," my child, "you have always been with me and what I have is yours" (v. 31). This father is not disconnected, it seems. He reminds the older son of his relationship with the younger when he says, "This brother of yours" (v. 32). He reminds him that brothers are family and can't be disconnected. He names the significance of the younger's return: he was lost and now found, he has come back home, back to life, back to God, back to family—to God's family and to salvation.

We might see that the father symbolizes God and the sons are two kind of sinners. We are the sons, and God is the father who meets us and rejoices at our return, our restoration. God gives us back our identity as a child of God. Does God have the same love for both sinners? It seems so. He meets both in the same way. So what does the property symbolize? It could be all of the benefits of being a child of God such as forgiveness, salvation, and blessing. The younger gives this up, but God is not fazed by our mess. Interesting, too, that neither son repents before the father acts.

God comes to them and meets them where they are.

Levine suggests that this parable is about families and fathers and how we treat each other and behave.[5] And don't we wonder where the mother is? Perhaps this story just tells us about humans and how we children seek fulfillment and rebel rather than seeking love at home. The result is that we become in need. We will end up hungry and at our lowest point. But like the father, God wants us to restore our lost children and restore the family.

---

5. Levine, *Short Stories by Jesus*, 74.

Is this parable about how God is? Or is this parable about who we are? Or both?

To answer this, let's remember that this parable is like the other lost and found parables. In this one, however, people are lost rather than things are lost. Both sons are lost in different spiritual ways. The younger son has to come to a realization in order to return, and God meets him. Does the older son ever come to a realization?

Perhaps looking at the context of the parable will help determine its purpose. Jesus is telling this parable in response to the Pharisees who have just asked what kind of teacher he is, that he eats with sinners and tax collectors. Such actions of Jesus show us that this is a God who loves and seeks sinners and tax collectors. It's as if Jesus says, "Yes, I eat with them because I come to seek the lost and bring them back into family—to make the family complete."

A few more thoughts:

Perhaps with the older son's anger, Jesus is acknowledging that we humans expect punishment for sins and rewards for obedience. That's how we do things, isn't it? But look at the father once more. Let's name verbs that describe his action and character.

The father:

- Gives abundantly
- Allows—no warning, threats, or questions
- Waits—indicates expectation
- Meets—with older son (God comes to him while he is angry or because he is angry, which is really hurt). Notice that this son does not turn.
- Demonstrates exuberant joy
- Celebrates
- Restores
- Saves

All of these actions one would only do for someone you love and value greatly.

And don't we see ourselves in the sons' actions? Yes, they are us. Like them, we:

- Are selfish
- Leave
- Are greedy

- Lack respect for God and family
- Seek fulfillment or worth in the world and, in turn, go against God's will, God's love, the law; we sin
- Turn and change only when we have nothing else

Or maybe we do the right thing and stay but only in order to get something. Our motives are selfish. We seek recognition and reward rather than give our obedience out of love and respect.

Both kinds of sinners (or sons) are dead and lost. These two states are equal: to be lost in this way is to be dead. But to be back in the family is to be found and to be alive, to be saved. So how does salvation come to them and restore them back into the family? We see then what kind of teacher Jesus is, eating with sinners, that God is meeting us where we are and restoring us to his children. Jesus, as God incarnate, as God with us, comes to the lost to find them and to the dead to bring them to life.

Step Three: Final Questions

What else do you see, observe, notice?

What was the loudest, most thought-provoking thing for you over this week of study?

What do you think and feel God is saying to you through this parable?

Does this insight move your heart toward some kind of repentance and renewal?

Conclusion

Perhaps these four weeks of contemplating and penetrating the parables have pricked your heart and moved you toward repentance and renewal. If so, then thanks be to God. We can imagine that such a feeling might be what Wesley called his heart "being strangely warmed" as he listened to Luther's commentary on that evening that changed his life.

My contention, among those asserted in the introduction to this study, is that our serious engagement with scripture, as we have attempted to do in these four weeks, will change our lives. Who knows what new and wonderful things God can do with us? Taking time to dig around in scripture and making time to pray demonstrate to God that we mean business, that our faith has legs. Intentionally and deliberately opening our hearts allows God to meet us where we are and for the Holy Spirit to do some "strange" warming of our hearts as well.

So I challenge you: Use the daily reading schedule that accompanies this study to read other biblical texts in the same way. Your continued serious engagement with scripture will continue to challenge and to provoke a positive change in your heart and move you further toward repentance and renewal.

Remember that the active and present God:

- Constantly reaches out to us who intentionally and willingly reach out to God;
- Desires a close and deep connection with you; and
- Strives to initiate your growth and change through our repentance and awareness so that we can bring God's love here on earth.

As I noted earlier, God wants nothing less for us than to move us out of our complacency into a dynamic, thriving, abundant wholeness for ourselves and for others—indeed, for the entire world.

Bibliography

Benner, David. *Opening to God: Lectio Divina and Life as Prayer.* Expanded ed. Downer's Grove: InterVarsity Press, 2021.

Craven, Toni, and Walter Harrelson. "The Psalms." In *The New Interpreter's Study Bible.* Nashville: Abingdon, 2003.

Freedman, David Noel, Allen C. Myers, and Astrid B. Beck, editors. *Eerdmans Dictionary of the Bible.* Grand Rapids, Mich.: Wm. B. Eerdmans, 2000. https://www.accordancebible.com

Gale, Aaron M. "The Gospel According to Matthew." In *The Jewish Annotated New Testament.* 2nd ed. Edited by Amy-Jill Levine and Marc Zvi Butler. New York: Oxford University Press, 2017.

Gallagher, Susan, and Roger Lundin. *Literature through the Eyes of Faith.* San Francisco: Harper, 1989.

Gesenius, H. F. W. *A Hebrew and English Lexicon of the Old Testament.* Edited by Francis Brown. Oxford: Oxford University Press, 1952. https://accordancebible.com.

Goodman, Daniel R. "On the Use of בֵל and Καρδία in the Old and New Testaments." *Journal of the Society of Biblical Literature and Exegesis,* no. 10. Jun-Dec 1881: 67-72.

Levine, Amy-Jill. *Short Stories by Jesus: The Enigmatic Parables of a Controversial Rabbi.* New York: Harper One, 2014.

Livingstone, E. A., ed. *The Oxford Concise Dictionary of the Christian Church.* 3rd ed. Oxford: Oxford University Press, 2013.

Nanos, Mark D. "The Letter of Paul to the Romans." In *The Jewish Annotated New Testament.* 2nd ed. Edited by Amy-Jill Levine and Marc Zvi Butler. New York: Oxford University Press, 2017.

Olson, Mark K. "John Wesley's Doctrine of the Holy Spirit." https://wesleyscholar.com. Accessed April 1, 2023.

Tolbert, Mary Ann. "The Gospel According to Mark." In *The New Interpreter's Study Bible*. Nashville: Abingdon Press, 2003.

About the Author

Suzan Phillips holds a master's degree in theology from Lutheran Theological Southern Seminary and a master's degree in English from Winthrop University. A former English professor and higher education administrator, Suzan plans to pursue a ministry of writing, teaching, and speaking. She is married to United Methodist elder the Rev. Charles Phillips, who as of this writing is appointed to First United Methodist Church on the Isle of Palms, South Carolina. They have two daughters, a son-in-law, a granddaughter, and a grandson on the way.

Made in the USA
Columbia, SC
29 April 2025

57290135R00036